AF270589

Stellar Space

History of NASA

by Julie Murray

Dash!
LEVELED READERS
An Imprint of Abdo Zoom • abdobooks.com
3

Level 1 – Beginning
Short and simple sentences with familiar words or patterns for children who are beginning to understand how letters and sounds go together.

Level 2 – Emerging
Longer words and sentences with more complex language patterns for readers who are practicing common words and letter sounds.

Level 3 – Transitional
More developed language and vocabulary for readers who are becoming more independent.

abdobooks.com

Published by Abdo Zoom, a division of ABDO, PO Box 398166, Minneapolis, Minnesota 55439.
Copyright © 2022 by Abdo Consulting Group, Inc. International copyrights reserved in all countries.
No part of this book may be reproduced in any form without written permission from the publisher.
Dash!™ is a trademark and logo of Abdo Zoom.

Printed in the United States of America, North Mankato, Minnesota.
052021
092021

Photo Credits: Alamy, iStock, NASA, Science Source, Shutterstock
Production Contributors: Kenny Abdo, Jennie Forsberg, Grace Hansen, John Hansen
Design Contributors: Candice Keimig, Neil Klinepier, Victoria Bates

Library of Congress Control Number: 2020919496

Publisher's Cataloging in Publication Data

Names: Murray, Julie, author.
Title: History of NASA / by Julie Murray
Description: Minneapolis, Minnesota : Abdo Zoom, 2022 | Series: Stellar space | Includes online resources and index.
Identifiers: ISBN 9781098226268 (lib. bdg.) | ISBN 9781098226404 (ebook) | ISBN 9781098226473 (Read-to-Me ebook)
Subjects: LCSH: Outer space--Juvenile literature. | Outer space--Exploration--Juvenile literature. | United States. National Aeronautics and Space Administration--Juvenile literature. | Astronautics--Juvenile literature. | Manned space flight--Juvenile literature.
Classification: DDC 629.4097--dc23

Table of Contents

The
Beginning
4

NASA stands for National Aeronautics and Space Administration. It is a US government agency. Its mission is to explore space and flight.

President Dwight D. Eisenhower established NASA on July 29, 1958. This was in response to Russia launching Sputnik 1. The US wanted to compete in the **Space Race**.

THE TEAM BEHIND THE SATURN
DIVISION SUPPORTING CONTRACTORS

Missions

On May 5, 1961, Alan Shepard became the first US astronaut in space. The Freedom 7 mission sent him 116 miles (187 km) into space. It lasted a little over 15 minutes.

10
TO REPOSITION
PUSH BUTTONS
FORWARD

NASA was first to put humans on the moon. Neil Armstrong and Buzz Aldrin landed on the moon on July 20, 1969. They spent more than 2.5 hours outside on the moon's surface.

NASA's **Space Shuttle Program** ran from 1981 to 2011. The program launched 135 missions. Two of its missions ended in disaster. Challenger broke apart shortly after takeoff. Columbia broke apart reentering Earth's **atmosphere**.

LIQUIFIED HYDROGEN
FLAMMABLE GAS

NASA has sent **rovers** into space. Its Lunar Roving Vehicle explored the moon's surface. Curiosity found elements on Mars needed to support life.

Launched in 1990, the Hubble Space Telescope has discovered new moons and **galaxies**. One of the most famous images it's captured is called the *Pillars of Creation*. It shows new stars forming.

NASA plays a big role in the
International Space Station (ISS).
The ISS is a large spacecraft
where astronauts can live. It is
also a science lab. Many countries
worked together to build it.

More than 240 people from 19 different countries have visited the ISS. NASA supports the ISS from the ground and in space.

NASA Today

NASA has overseen more than 1,200 missions. These flights have helped us better understand our universe. Today, NASA continues to explore space and share its discoveries with the world!

NASA Facts

- Has landed many successful missions on the moon and Mars, with more planned

- Has flown mice, frogs, and monkeys into space

- Has over 80 current missions

- More than 17,000 people work for NASA

- More than 350 astronauts have trained with NASA since the 1960s

- Has about 50 active astronauts

Glossary

atmosphere – the gases surrounding the earth or similar objects in outer space.

galaxy – a collection of billions of stars and other matter held together by gravity. Our planet Earth and the sun belong to the Milky Way galaxy.

rover – a type of vehicle designed to travel on the surface of a planet, comet, or moon, for the purpose of providing transportation or retrieving data.

Space Race – the competition between nations regarding space exploration.

Space Shuttle program – a human spaceflight program organized by NASA which carried out routine transportation of crews and cargo into space from 1981 to 2011.

Index

Online Resources

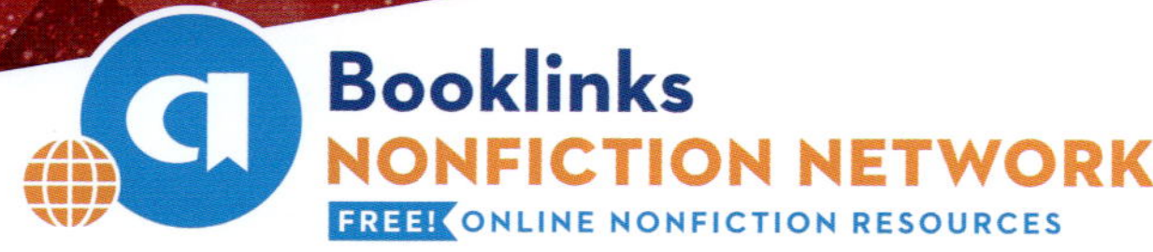

To learn more about the history of NASA, please visit **abdobooklinks.com** or scan this QR code. These links are routinely monitored and updated to provide the most current information available.